A Young Boy Named David
Book 7: Young and Tough

Written By: David M. Smith

Copyright

The "A Young Boy Named David" series is owned by Kingdom Being Consultants, LLC. No part of this publication may be reproduced, stored in a retrieval system, or transmitted in any way or by any means, either electronically, mechanically, by photocopy, recording, or any other method, without the prior authorization by the author, except as provided by US copyright law. This book is designed to provide accurate and authoritative information with regard to the subject matter covered. This information is given with the understanding that neither the author, nor Kingdom Being Consultants, LLC, is attempting to render legal or professional advice. The opinions expressed by the author are not necessarily those of Kingdom Being Consultants, LLC.

Copyright 2022 by David Smith
Library of Congress Control Number: 2022909307
ISBN: 9798821451606

Dear Young Reader,

Thank you for your support! I hope that my story helps you to deal with any pain that you are going through.

My goal is to help you to realize that you deserve to be happy. That is why I have written this special book...just for you! I have poured out my heart into these words.

This book is based on things that really happened to me. Please know that if you ever need help, you should go to a mature adult and let them know what's going on. Also, you've always got a friend in me!

Your Friend in Life,

David M. Smith

Dedication

I dedicate this book to God, my family, and any young boy or girl out there who needs to feel loved. We all have a story. Don't be afraid to share yours.

***

Feel free to invite David M. Smith for speaking, teaching, class appearances, conference keynotes, book studies, book signings, and workshops: www.d-m-smith.org

Characters

- David – me
- Leon – bully
- Mr. Butler
- Rhonda
- James Johnson
- James Wilkinson
- Mr. B, Mrs. B, and Baby B – family of rulers (you'll see)

Table of Contents

Chapter 1: Where My Fighting Started

My fighting history in school dates all the way back to pre-K. The portable building where my mom dropped me off and left me in that strange place. I was so very afraid, the first time around any kids and this weird feeling started creeping up in me.

"Please mom! Don't leave me here!" I begged her. But she did. I looked around at all the faces of these kids that I didn't know, and I just felt so angry about the whole thing. There was a big chubby kid that sat in front of me, and he was the class bully. Because he was bigger than everyone else, he would take our toys and push us around. I couldn't wait to get back home and away from this scary kid.

I was being bullied before I even knew what that meant. Then one day, Leon (the bully) walked up and took away my favorite box of crayons. "These are mine now!" he growled. To my surprise, and to everyone else's, I got so mad at this that I pulled back and whopped Leon so hard that he fell over and hit his face on a desk! We couldn't believe it! Little David had taken down the big bad bully! The amount of respect and fear I got from the other kids in the class became something I was determined to have all throughout my school days.

Fast forward to the fourth grade, and I had become a young and tough boy ready to act up and show out! Not having any guidance in my life was causing my behavior to go down the drain. That's what happens when there's no adult taking an interest in raising you to be a good person. Have you gone through this? I hope not. But if so, I pray that one of your teachers steps up to fill this role for you. This happened to me with Mr. Butler. I'll tell you more about him later. For now, I have some more stories to tell about the beginning of my school fighting career!

In Mr. Butler's class, there were 14 students. All were boys, except for Rhonda, the only girl in the group. "You boys don't scare me at all! Don't try to mess with me, or I'll pop you in the head!" she declared to all of us one day. I stood up and said, "we aren't afraid of no girl! Bring it on, Rho-" POP!!! You guessed it...I got popped in the head by Rhonda! As tough as my life at home was making me, I knew to leave Rhonda alone! In fact, we actually became close friends after this. Really, Rhonda was cool with all the guys in the class. Even though she still sucked her thumb, she had proven her toughness, and we never teased her about it.

Now to tell you about Mr. Butler. I can still remember the first day in his class. "Alright kids. Listen up," he said to all of us in his big booming voice. I tried to listen, but I was distracted by his size and full beard and mustache. He continued, "this is my class, and I'm the one in charge. Don't you forget it. Let me introduce you to my family." He then went up to the board and grabbed three rulers.

"Say hello to Mr. B, Mrs. B, and Baby B." All three rulers were different sizes, and he said that he would only have to use them if we acted up or got out of hand. Let's just say that I became very familiar with Mr. Butler's "family"!

Mr. Butler had an interesting way of dealing with us. It turns out that all the rough and troubled kids got sent to his class. And we all had built up anger and stress from our lives at home, which meant we were always getting into fights. Here's what's crazy…*Mr. Butler would let us fight!* This created a system among us. The kids who were good fighters and won a lot were the ones who were seen as the top class, the kids you didn't mess with.

Right away, they could tell that I would fight. "You know why they call me

Monster Mash?" I said, trying to brag to my classmates. "Why?" a kid named James said. "Because a monster mashed you in the head and made you stupid?" This got a huge laugh out of everyone. But all it did was make me very angry. "No, James, it's because if you mash the wrong button, I'll go monster all over your dumb self!"

Well, James had officially challenged me in front of everyone. I could tell that he wanted to take the spot as the number one tough guy. Little did I know that this would lead to an intense battle between him and me to find out who was really the toughest in Mr. Butler's class!

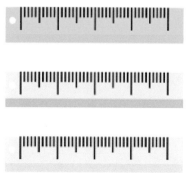

Chapter 2: A Boy Named James

I don't know what James was going through in his life, but I do know that this was a very dark time in my life. I was so full of anger at home because of my mom's problems getting worse, my brother ditching me for his new friends, and seeing so many terrible accidents with my own two eyes. So when I got to school, I was already in a mean, fighting mood, and anything could set me over the edge. I had developed a temper. I would go off fast on someone. Usually, it was James Johnson who I fought the most. Which was surprising when you realize that James was a really big guy! In fact, we called him the Incredible Hulk because when he got angry his face would get dark and he would sometimes break things.

But that didn't scare me. I was just mad that he tried to be a bully and take over the classroom. Back in those days, I was ready to fight just about anyone!

"Come on guys, who do you think would win in a fight...a Monster or a

Hulk?" James asked the class one day. I remember us all standing by the door, probably because class was almost over. Something came over me, and I just snapped. "Why don't you stop asking and come fight me to find out?" I yelled. That started my first real fight in school! James came rushing at me full force. My eyes got big. I didn't expect him to come at me so hard! "David, look out!" Rhonda cried out, but it was too late. James, as tall as he was, got to me in just two steps, lifted me up, and was trying to squeeze the life out of me, like I was a lemon!

"Let me go!" I struggled to say. Then I raised my hand back and knocked James right in the face. BAM! BAM! I hit him twice, and he fell back and let me go. I hit him hard enough to make him run to the back of the classroom and stop trying to out-tough me. Mr. Butler, who had been watching the whole fight go down, stood up and said, "well, now that you guys got that out of your system, maybe we can start acting a bit more civilized." Wow! There's no way a teacher would have that reaction nowadays. I actually don't like the idea of kids fighting in school. In the end, you don't prove anything, and you just end up getting hurt.

I don't want you guys to fight like I did. If you have problems at home or have issues with someone in your class, go to one of your counselors for help. That way, you might avoid going through what happened in my next fight. Interestingly enough, it was with another kid named James!

Chapter 3: The Other James

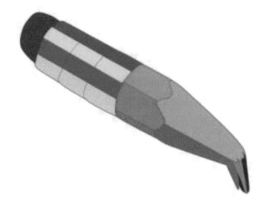

My fights continued, and it seemed like everyone named James had it out for me! I was definitely angrier at this other James, because that day in class, James Wilkinson brought up my brother's death. "Hey David? Whatever happened to your little brother, huh? Where are you guys hiding him?" he said one day. I couldn't believe what I heard him say. "James. Be very careful about what you say next," I said in a low, angry voice. "Awww, the little baby Monster Mash is gonna cry! Hahaha!"

At this, some of the other kids began laughing with James, and I could no longer hold back my feelings. I loved my brother Larry so much, and when we lost him to a disease, it made me go into a very dark place. Now, it was being brought up as a rude joke, and people were laughing at him. What was I supposed to do?

I'll tell you what…I should have gone to a teacher. When you're upset like that, you need an adult to help you make a good decision. That will prevent you from doing something violent or mean, which will only make the situation worse anyways.

Also, from the viewpoint of James, please know that it's never good to make fun of someone's family, especially someone they have lost. The pain of that loss can activate emotions in that person that are hard for them to control. And boy, is that what happened to me!

"James, I'm going to tell you one more time. Stop. Talking. About. My. Brother!!" I was standing up this time, staring him down with the meanest glare I could come up with. It didn't work. "Why doesn't your brother come over here and stop me? Oh, right! He can't, because he's-"

I didn't dare let him finish that sentence. I had been drawing at my desk, so my pencil was nearby. I grabbed it and ran up to James. He was still laughing at his dumb "joke", so he didn't see me coming.

I raised my hand back, put all my force into it, and slammed it down into his shoulder! You have never heard a little boy scream and yell so loud! Of all the fights we had in Mr. Butler's class, this one made him leap out of his seat and get involved. I guess he drew the line at breaking off a pencil in a kid's shoulder! "David Smith! What in the world did you do??" he shouted at me. Forget Mr. B, Mrs. B, or Baby B...he looked mad enough to come at me all by himself!

SCHOOL
NURSE

James ended up in the nurse's office, and I was sent home and not allowed to come back to school for the rest of the week. I don't want you to react to situations the way I did. But I can tell you that no one ever made fun of Little Larry again!

Next Time...

Like I've said already, fighting is never the answer. But at that time in my life, it's all I knew how to do. My anger was growing and growing, and the only people I felt like I could take it out on were my classmates. Because I was so tough, I won many of my fights. But I quickly learned that you can't win them all! Come back next time to hear about some of the battles that didn't turn out the way I had hoped! And remember, we all have our own stories. Don't be afraid to tell yours!

Questions to Discuss

1. How did you feel when your parents left you at school for the first time?

2. Do you think it was right for Mr. Butler to let his students fight each other?

3. Have you ever been bullied like David was? How did it make you feel?

4. Is it right to make fun of someone's dead family member?

5. Was it right for David to fight back when he was upset?

Made in the USA
Columbia, SC
21 November 2024

46773178R00015